NDER THE
ICROSCOPE

VIRUSES UP CLOSE

BY JOHN SHEA

Gareth Stevens
Publishing

Please visit our website, www.garethstevens.com. For a free color catalog of all our high-quality books, call toll free 1-800-542-2595 or fax 1-877-542-2596.

Library of Congress Cataloging-in-Publication Data

Shea, John M.
Viruses up close / John M. Shea, M.D.
    pages cm. — (Under the microscope)
Includes index.
ISBN 978-1-4339-8355-9 (pbk.)
ISBN 978-1-4339-8356-6 (6-pack)
ISBN 978-1-4339-8354-2 (library binding)
1. Viruses—Juvenile literature. 2. Virus diseases—Juvenile literature. I. Title.
QR365.S54 2014
614.5'8—dc23

                                    2012047240

First Edition

Published in 2014 by
Gareth Stevens Publishing
111 East 14th Street, Suite 349
New York, NY 10003

Copyright © 2014 Gareth Stevens Publishing

Designer: Katelyn E. Reynolds
Editor: Therese Shea

Photo credits: Cover, p. 1 Visuals Unlimited, Inc./Volker Brinkmann/Getty Images; cover, pp. 1, 3–31 (logo and virus image icons) iStockphoto/Thinkstock.com; cover, pp. 1–31 (virus image icon) ramcreations/Shutterstock.com; cover, pp. 1–31 (virus image icon) Andrii Muzyka/Shutterstock.com; cover, pp. 1–31 (virus image icon) Lightspring/ Shutterstock.com; cover, pp. 1–32 (background texture) Hemera/Thinkstock.com; pp. 5, 16, 18 iStockphoto/Thinkstock.com; p. 7 After Frank Hancox/The Bridgeman Art Library/Getty Images; p. 8 BSIP/UIG via Getty Images; p. 9 Valérie75/Wikipedia.com; p. 11 MedicalRF.com/Getty Images; p. 13 Martin Shields/Photo Researchers/Getty Images; p. 15 Dept. of Microbiology, Biozentrum/Science Photo Library/Getty Images; pp. 17, 20, 21 Chris Bjornberg/Photo Researchers/Getty Images; p. 19 Lee D. Simon/Photo Researchers/Getty Images; p. 23 Science Source-CDC/Photo Researchers/Getty Images; p. 25 Visuals Unlimited, Inc./Carol & Mike Werner/Getty Images; p. 26 CandyBox Images/ Shutterstock.com; p. 27 George Musil/Visuals Unlimited/Getty Images; p. 29 (illustrations) Dorling Kindersley RF/Thinkstock.com.

Printed in the United States of America

CPSIA compliance information: Batch #CS13GS: For further information contact Gareth Stevens, New York, New York at 1-800-542-2595.

CONTENTS

Words in the glossary appear in **bold** type the first time they are used in the text.

THE HIDDEN
WORLD OF GERMS

We all get sick. Sometimes, it's a runny nose or a sore throat that we may find annoying. Or we may get a fever, headaches, and muscle aches that make it difficult to get out of bed and go to school. Some people may become so ill that their heart or lungs don't work as well as they should. These life-threatening illnesses require hospitalization and medications to keep the patient alive.

Some of these conditions are called infectious diseases because one person can infect, or spread the disease to, another person. Common causes of infectious diseases include viruses. Viruses are so tiny that only the most powerful microscopes can see them, and yet some have the ability to hurt or even kill us.

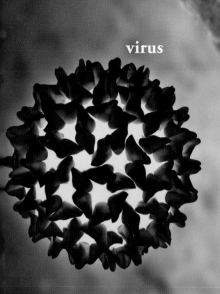
virus

HOW SMALL ARE
VIRUSES?

Most viruses range in size from 20 to 300 nanometers in **diameter**. (There are 10 million nanometers in a centimeter.) In comparison, the smallest human cells have a diameter of about 10,000 nanometers. This size is difficult to imagine, but consider that over 50 million virus particles can fit into a single human cell! Just recently, the largest virus ever described, the Megavirus, was discovered off the coast of Chile in 2011. It's 700 nanometers in diameter.

cell

The cells of the human body are tiny. A light microscope is needed to see them clearly. However, these cells are large compared to most viruses. Light microscopes can see none but the largest viruses.

AN EXTREMELY SMALL DISCOVERY

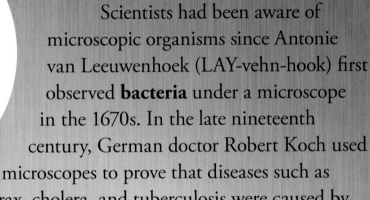

Scientists had been aware of microscopic organisms since Antonie van Leeuwenhoek (LAY-vehn-hook) first observed **bacteria** under a microscope in the 1670s. In the late nineteenth century, German doctor Robert Koch used microscopes to prove that diseases such as anthrax, cholera, and tuberculosis were caused by bacteria. At this time, scientists were beginning to understand that very small organisms could cause health problems.

In 1892, Russian scientist Dmitry Ivanovsky made an important discovery. He had been studying diseases in tobacco plants. He took parts of a diseased tobacco plant and passed it through a filter that would block even the smallest bacteria. Surprisingly, what did pass through caused healthy plants to become diseased. It seemed that something much smaller than bacteria caused infectious diseases, too.

VIRUSES AND LIGHT
MICROSCOPES

Early scientists who studied viruses were limited by their tools. Even today, the smallest **resolution** most light microscopes can achieve is about 200 nanometers, which is larger than most viruses. In comparison, the resolution of the unaided human eye is about 100,000 nanometers. New light microscopes that can see objects 50 nanometers across are now being developed. These powerful tools will allow scientists to study how viruses behave as they infect living cells.

Robert Koch was one of the first people to link tiny microscopic bacteria with certain diseases. Researchers today still use his theories when studying causes of infectious diseases.

7

BENEFICIAL VIRUSES?

Scientists have known for a while that some bacteria are actually good for human health. Some bacteria make vitamins in our guts or help keep away more harmful bacteria. Many researchers wonder if helpful viruses exist, too. Viruses such as the hepatitis A virus or the cytomegalovirus may help decrease damage done by more harmful viruses. One virus, Seneca Valley Virus-001, actually kills cancer cells more effectively than traditional cancer-fighting drugs.

In addition to proving the existence of the yellow fever virus, Walter Reed and James Carroll showed that the virus was spread by the bite of a mosquito. They proved this when Carroll was bitten by a mosquito that fed first on infected patients!

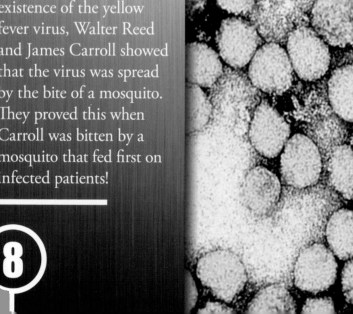

A few years later, in 1898, further evidence appeared that unseen substances could cause disease, this time in animals. Scientist Friedrich Loeffler had been an assistant to Robert Koch. He and Dr. Paul Frosch studied the causes of foot-and-mouth disease, a serious and deadly illness that affects farm animals. Similar to Ivanovsky, the team used filters to show that something much smaller than bacteria could spread foot-and-mouth disease among animals.

Despite these interesting discoveries, some people didn't believe tiny microorganisms, the things we now call germs, had anything to do with human diseases. Convincing proof came in 1900, presented by a group of scientists including US Army doctor Walter Reed. The group was researching yellow fever, an often-fatal disease marked by high fever. They showed that yellow fever was caused by a germ that could pass through filters that stopped bacteria.

Dr. James Carroll
(1854–1907)

WHAT IS A VIRUS?

When Germans Max Knoll and Ernst Ruska invented the transmission electron microscope (TEM) around 1932, a powerful new tool became available to help us understand what tiny germs are. Ernst's brother Helmut Ruska was a medical doctor and among the first to use the TEM to see a virus and study its structure. As **techniques** using the TEM became better, scientists developed a fuller understanding of what a virus is made of and how it causes diseases.

All viruses are made up of at least two parts: **nucleic acid** and a layer of **protein**, called a capsid, that surrounds and protects the nucleic acid. Some viruses have a third part, called an envelope, which is a layer of **lipids** and proteins surrounding the capsid. The envelope helps the virus enter cells.

VIROIDS AND PRIONS

With only two or three parts, viruses are among the simplest infectious particles in nature. But there are even simpler germs. Viroids are composed of just nucleic acid and have no protein capsid. Viroids mainly cause diseases in plants, although there's some evidence that they can also cause infection in human livers. Prions are made of only proteins and have no nucleic acid. They're the infectious agent responsible for Creutzfeldt-Jakob disease, also called mad cow disease.

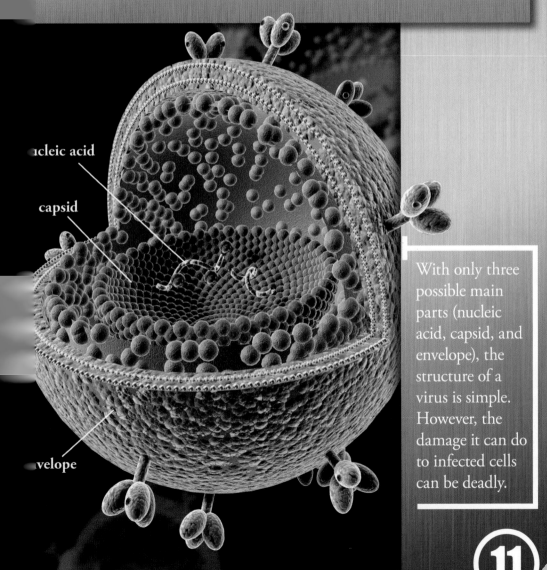

nucleic acid

capsid

envelope

With only three possible main parts (nucleic acid, capsid, and envelope), the structure of a virus is simple. However, the damage it can do to infected cells can be deadly.

NUCLEIC ACID

The innermost part of the virus contains nucleic acid. Nucleic acid is made from molecules called **nucleotides**. Nucleotides attach to one another like beads on a string. The order of the nucleotides forms a code, just like the order of letters in a book forms words and sentences. All life on this planet uses this code to grow and make copies of itself.

The two types of nucleic acid found in nature are deoxyribonucleic acid (DNA) and ribonucleic acid (RNA). Unlike most living things, which contain both DNA and RNA, viruses contain only one or the other. The nucleic acid in a virus contains the code, or the instructions, needed to make copies of that virus's parts, including more nucleic acid.

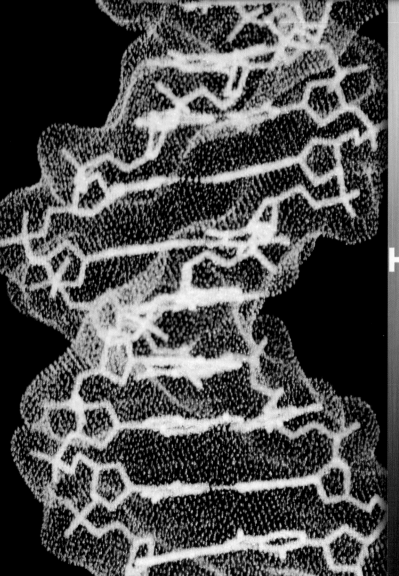

DNA AND RNA

In each cell, DNA acts like a library. It stores information in a central area. When the cell needs certain information (for example, if it needs to make more proteins), it copies the necessary information from DNA to RNA, much like making copies of pages in a book. The cell then follows the instructions on the RNA, while keeping the original information in DNA safe.

Nucleic acid is the **genetic** material of the virus. It contains the information the virus needs to make copies of itself.

THE PROTEIN CAPSID

Proteins provide structure and do the work needed for life. A shell made of proteins, the capsid, surrounds the nucleic acid in a virus. Just like the surface of a soccer ball is made up of smaller shapes that fit together, a capsid is made up of small repeating shapes that give the virus its larger overall structure.

A virus's nucleic acid stores the instructions to make the capsid's proteins out of chains of **amino acids**. The number of different proteins a virus contains depends on the type of virus, but most function with many less than other forms of life. Because of this, a virus doesn't have much nucleic acid and can remain small. In comparison, a human cell needs many kinds of proteins and so its DNA must be longer.

14

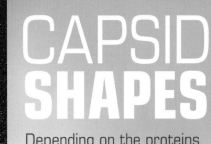

CAPSID
SHAPES

Depending on the proteins in the capsid shell, viruses come in an amazing variety of shapes. One common shape is helical, which means the nucleic acid is surrounded by a hollow cylinder or tube. Other viruses are polyhedral, which is a shape with multiple sides. Many such viruses are icosahedrons (20 sided). Some viruses are irregularly shaped and are referred to as binal, or complex, viruses.

Viral capsids come in many different sizes and shapes. This virus has a "tail" that helps it infect bacteria.

THE ENVELOPE

DID YOU KNOW?

Some viruses, such as the hepatitis B virus, have the lipid called cholesterol in their envelope. For reasons scientists don't understand yet, the presence of cholesterol is necessary for this virus to enter host cells.

Besides the two features found in all viruses—nucleic acid and a protein capsid—some viruses also have a viral envelope around the capsid. It's composed of proteins and lipids. Those viruses that don't have an envelope are called "naked." While the instructions to make proteins are stored in the nucleic acid, a virus doesn't contain any information about how to make the lipids of the envelope. It doesn't need to. The virus steals a portion of the **membrane** of the cell it infects, called the host cell. Some of the proteins on the viral envelope come from the host as well. The virus replaces them with some of its own proteins. Many viruses also grow spikes on their envelopes that help them attach to cell surfaces.

influenza virus

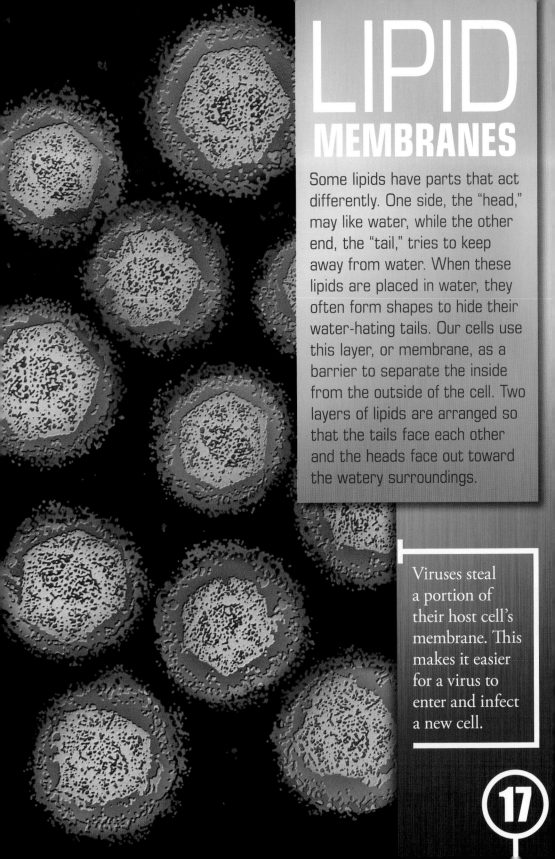

LIPID
MEMBRANES

Some lipids have parts that act differently. One side, the "head," may like water, while the other end, the "tail," tries to keep away from water. When these lipids are placed in water, they often form shapes to hide their water-hating tails. Our cells use this layer, or membrane, as a barrier to separate the inside from the outside of the cell. Two layers of lipids are arranged so that the tails face each other and the heads face out toward the watery surroundings.

Viruses steal a portion of their host cell's membrane. This makes it easier for a virus to enter and infect a new cell.

HOW DO VIRUSES WORK?

DID YOU KNOW?

Plants have cell walls that make it difficult for viruses to cross. Nearly all plant viruses depend on insects and other organisms that feed on plants to help them infect plant cells.

Viruses are **parasites**. They depend on living cells to make copies of, or replicate, themselves. The virus provides the cell instructions in the form of nucleic acid, while the cell provides the energy and the building material. Unfortunately, the virus harms the cell as it replicates.

A virus follows a process to replicate itself. First, it finds a suitable host cell. In the step called adsorption, the virus attaches itself to the outer surface of the host cell. In the next step, called penetration, the virus gets past the membrane of the host cell. In some cases, the virus's envelope allows it to slide through the membrane. In other cases, the virus tricks the cell into creating an opening to allow the virus to enter.

CELL RECEPTORS

Human cells have special molecules, called receptors, on their outside membrane that are important for the cell's health. These receptors aid cells in communicating and interacting with each other. Viruses often use these receptors to their benefit. Proteins on the viral capsid or envelope turn on receptors, much like a key opens a lock. This triggers a process in which the cell brings the receptor (along with the attached virus) inside.

The first step in viral replication is the virus's attachment to the host cell's membrane, followed by its penetration into the host cell.

ARE VIRUSES ALIVE?

While viruses share much in common with living organisms (including the presence of nucleic acid and proteins), they're missing much of the cellular machinery that some scientists insist is essential for life. Outside of a host cell, a virus cannot replicate or produce energy. Because of this, scientists disagree whether viruses are truly alive. However, nearly all scientists agree that viruses play an important role in shaping life on Earth.

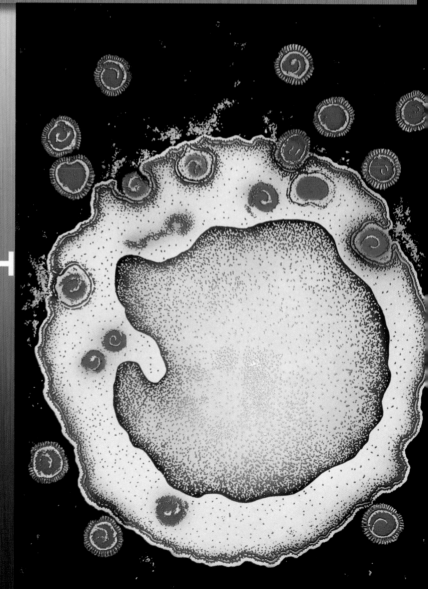

Once inside its host cell, a virus takes control and directs the cell to make more copies of its proteins and nucleic acid.

What happens once the virus gets inside the host depends on the type of virus and the type of host cell. In most cases, the virus undergoes the uncoating process. During this stage, the protein capsid breaks down, releasing the virus's nucleic acid. Then, the code contained in the viral nucleic acid instructs the cell to start making the proteins needed to make virus parts. The cell also makes copies of the viral nucleic acid.

The next step is the maturation phase, also called the assembly phase. Viral proteins move into a certain area of the cell. There, capsid shells are built around the newly made viral nucleic acid. More than 10,000 new virus particles can be made in a host cell that was infected with just one virus!

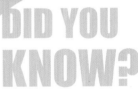

DID YOU KNOW?

In addition to providing instructions for its capsid, viral nucleic acid may also contain instructions to make proteins called enzymes that help the virus replicate and assemble.

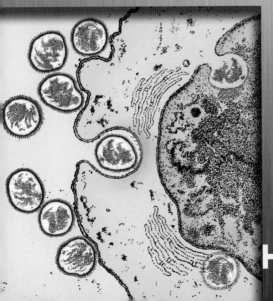

avian flu virus infecting a cell

VIRAL RELEASE

Viruses have different ways of exiting the host cell. The most common way for naked viruses (viruses without envelopes) to exit is to burst open the cell membrane from the inside. This process, called lysis, leads to the death of the host cell.

One strategy used by enveloped viruses is a process called budding. The virus pushes out of the host cell, forming a little bud. It takes some of the cell's membrane as it finally leaves. Some viruses obtain their envelope from other cell structures, such as the nucleus, before being transported outside. In many cases, the host cell may not die, but rather continues to slowly release new viral particles into the outside environment.

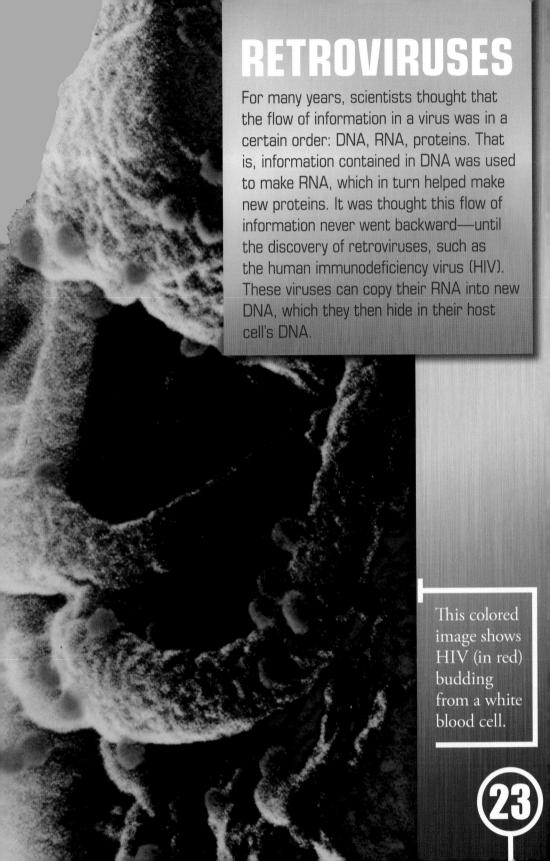

RETROVIRUSES

For many years, scientists thought that the flow of information in a virus was in a certain order: DNA, RNA, proteins. That is, information contained in DNA was used to make RNA, which in turn helped make new proteins. It was thought this flow of information never went backward—until the discovery of retroviruses, such as the human immunodeficiency virus (HIV). These viruses can copy their RNA into new DNA, which they then hide in their host cell's DNA.

This colored image shows HIV (in red) budding from a white blood cell.

COMMON HUMAN VIRUSES

Almost everyone is familiar with the common cold and its symptoms of runny nose, sore throat, and cough. There are over 200 different types of viruses that cause colds in people! The rhinovirus is the most common, causing about one-third of all colds. Rhinoviruses grow best at 91ºF (38ºC), which is about the temperature inside the human nose. (*Rhin* is Greek for "nose.")

Influenza, or flu, affects between 5 and 20 percent of people each year. Symptoms usually include cough, fever, and muscle aches. The influenza virus is constantly changing, and many new types of influenza viruses have appeared over the years, some of them deadly. This makes the influenza virus unpredictable and scary. The "Spanish flu" of 1918 and 1919 was responsible for over 50 million deaths.

ANTIBODIES

When our bodies encounter viruses, bacteria, or even some poisons, our immune system responds by making antibodies. These Y-shaped proteins are produced by white blood cells. Antibodies can attach to a viral capsid or envelope, which prevents the virus from entering and infecting any cells. It may take days or weeks for the body to start making the correct antibodies to a virus. However, once it does, those antibodies can protect against that infection for decades.

Washing your hands often and covering your mouth and nose when you sneeze and cough are the best defense against spreading germs. However, antibodies (shown here at work) help when you do get a virus.

25

VACCINES

Vaccines are medications that usually contain a weakened part of a germ. When someone is given a vaccine, they make antibodies to target that germ. When the vaccinated person is exposed later to a stronger version of the germ, their body is ready to stop the infection. The smallpox virus has been responsible for millions of deaths throughout history. However, because of a successful vaccination program, there hasn't been a case of smallpox in more than 35 years.

The varicella-zoster virus can cause two different diseases, chickenpox and shingles. Since 1995, most school-age children receive a vaccination against the varicella-zoster virus to prevent chickenpox.

Chickenpox is a disease marked by itchy blisters covering the whole body. It's normally a mild disease among young children, but it can be very serious for older adults who catch it. In many cases, chickenpox goes away by itself, but the varicella-zoster virus can sometimes hide inside nerve cells. The virus can become active again later and cause shingles, which is a painful, burning rash on the skin.

Warts are small growths on the skin. They're caused by human papillomavirus and can be spread from person to person or from one part of the body to another. There are over 100 types of human papillomaviruses, each of which seems specialized in infecting a specific body location.

varicella-zoster virus

THE FUTURE OF VIRAL RESEARCH

We have learned much about viruses and how they work over the past century, but there's still much to learn. Unfortunately, new viruses are appearing every year. Severe acute respiratory syndrome (SARS) is a serious and deadly form of **pneumonia**. The SARS coronavirus rapidly spread across the globe in 2003. It was responsible for about 8,000 infections and 750 deaths.

Studying how viruses work gives doctors better tools to treat viral infections. Because viruses use our own cells to replicate, it's hard to make a medicine that won't harm our cells while destroying the virus. Finding out about each virus's characteristics gives researchers better targets for designing new and more effective antiviral medicines.

OW A VIRUS REPLICATES

ADSORPTION
The virus attaches to a host cell.

PENETRATION
Some enveloped viruses pass through the cell membrane. Other viruses trick cells into allowing them to enter.

UNCOATING
Once inside, the capsid breaks down and releases the viral nucleic acid. The nucleic acid starts to take control of the cell.

REPLICATION AND MATURATION
The viral nucleic acid instructs the host cell to make capsid proteins and more viral nucleic acids. The proteins assemble into new capsid shells around viral nucleic acids.

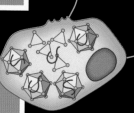

RELEASE
Viruses can burst open a cell in a process called lysis. Other viruses leave their host cells by budding and stealing a portion of the cell membrane for their envelope.

VIRUSES AND CANCER

Understanding how viruses work not only helps us fight infections, it can help fight some cancers as well. Scientists from the World Health Organization estimate that more than 10 percent of cancers are caused by an infection, such as certain types of human papillomavirus and some hepatitis viruses. Fortunately, vaccines are available to prevent some of these infections and therefore prevent these cancers.

GLOSSARY

amino acid: a small molecule that is a building block of proteins

bacteria: tiny creatures that can only be seen with a microscope

diameter: the distance from one side of a round object to another through its center

electron: a tiny particle in atoms. An electron microscope uses a beam of electrons to create an image of a microscopic object.

genetic: relating to genes, the tiny parts of a cell that are passed along during reproduction

lipid: a type of chemical that doesn't mix well with water. Lipids include fats and cholesterol.

membrane: a thin tissue in the body

nucleic acid: a substance present in living cells and viruses that has molecules consisting of many nucleotides linked in a long chain. DNA and RNA are nucleic acids.

nucleotide: a compound that forms the basic unit of nucleic acid

parasite: something that lives in, on, or with another living thing and obtains benefits while harming the host

pneumonia: an infection of the lungs

protein: a structural material made by the body

resolution: a measure of the sharpness of an image

technique: the method, skill, or art used to perform a task

FOR MORE INFORMATION

BOOKS

Biskup, Agnieszka. *Understanding Viruses with Max Axiom, Super Scientist*. Mankato, MN: Capstone Press, 2009.

Herbst, Judith. *Germ Theory*. Minneapolis, MN: Twenty-First Century Books, 2008.

Landau, Elaine. *The Common Cold*. New York, NY: Marshall Cavendish Benchmark, 2009.

WEBSITES

All the Virology on the WWW
www.virology.net/atvimages.html
This website provides links for many virus-related sites, including a large and interesting collection of viral images.

Centers for Disease Control and Prevention
www.cdc.gov
The CDC is a world leader in infectious disease research, and its website contains information on new and important diseases.

INDEX